T5-AQA-756

BEST FOOT FORWARD

THE COMPLETE GUIDE TO OBEDIENCE HANDLING

by Barbara S. Handler

1984

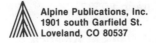
Alpine Publications, Inc.
1901 south Garfield St.
Loveland, CO 80537

This book is dedicated to:

My dogs, who made it possible;
My students, who made it necessary.

Cover photo: Ch. Bournedale's Prospector C.D.X. performs the broad jump for owner Tim Read. (Photo by the author.)

Credits   Cover design: Leanne Mason
Layout: Susan Allard
Typesetting: Hope Hicks, Artline

ISBN No. 0-931866-20-0

Copyright © 1984 by Barbara Handler.

All rights reserved. No part of this book may be used or reproduced in any form without written permission from the publisher except in cases of brief quotations embodied in critical articles and reviews. For information address: Alpine Publications, Inc., 214 19th Street S.E., Loveland, Colorado 80537.

Printed in the United States of America.

Contents

Contents

Introduction

Obedience Trials are a sport and all participants should be guided by the principals of good sportsmanship both in and outside of the ring. The purpose of Obedience Trials is to demonstrate the usefulness of the pure-bred dog as a companion of man, not merely the dog's ability to follow specified routines in the obedience ring. While all contestants in a class are required to perform the same exercises in substantially the same way so that the relative quality of the various performances may be compared and scored, the basic objective of Obedience Trials is to produce dogs that have been trained and conditioned always to behave in the home, in public places, and in the presence of other dogs, in a manner that will reflect credit on the sport of Obedience. The performance of dog and handler in the ring must be accurate and correct and must conform to the requirements of these Regulations. However, it is also essential that the dog demonstrate willingness and enjoyment of its work, and that smoothness and naturalness on the part of the handler be given precedence over a performance based on military precision and peremptory commands.

American Kennel Club
Obedience Regulations
September 1, 1982

People show their dogs in obedience trials for many different reasons - to have a tangible reward (a ribbon, a trophy, a certificate) for all of the months they have spent training; to compete for local awards and placements in national rating systems; for the fun and companionship with both the dogs and the people; or for a personal sense of satisfaction. Whatever your reasons, it is vital that you have a fairly clear view of your goals before you enter your dog in an obedience trial. Setting your sights realistically involves understanding your dog's limitations and your own level of commitment of time and energy.

A dog who can perform all of the required exercises is generally a delightful house pet, but an obedience trial is a formal competition and an artificial situation and therefore, the exercises must be done in a particular manner. The rules for competition are spelled out in *Obedience Regulations*, available free from the American Kennel Club, 51 Madison Avenue, New York, New York, 10010. Every potential exhibitor should be familiar with this small booklet. There are, however, some unwritten rules which do not appear in that publication, as well as many ideas about handling and show preparation developed by experienced participants over the years which may prove helpful to both new and experienced exhibitors. These are the subject of this book.

Best Foot Forward is meant to serve as an aid to the person who is already familiar with the basic requirements for the obedience exercises—it is not a training manual to teach the dog how to perform the exercises. It is designed to fit with any training program and is especially useful for the individual who trains alone, without the benefit of a class situation or the advice of an experienced instructor.

DEFINING YOUR GOALS

Success is a word we each define differently. For one exhibitor success may mean winning a placement in a class, or achieving a particularly high score. The same handler, with a more difficult dog, may be thrilled simply to qualify and to have verification that the dog is truly under control. Some people are competitive by nature; others are not. If you are going to enjoy the world of obedience training and exhibiting, you must set goals that are meaningful for you. Train to please yourself and don't feel you must have the same orientation to obedience exhibiting as any other person. You must also maintain a realistic perspective of your dog's abilities. It is fine to expect your dog to give you his best (assuming, of course, that you have done your best as a trainer), but not every dog is capable of achieving top scores. Be honest in your assessment and be satisfied with your dog's best efforts, no matter what score he earns.

ELIGIBILITY

Is your dog eligible for AKC obedience trials? The answer is yes, if you own a registered purebred of one of the AKC recognized breeds (or one for whom you have secured an Indefinite Listing Privilege number), and if the dog has not been artifically altered *in any manner not customary for its breed*. That means that it is okay to show your tail-less Pembroke Welsh Corgi, but not your tail-less Labrador Retriever, unless the Lab was born that way. If your dog has been noticeably surgically altered because of an accident, he may not compete. Ethically, he should be removed from competition if he has had any surgical alteration other than spaying, castration or debarking, even if the results are not visible. Dogs who have been neutered and/or debarked are eligible to compete.

If your dog does not meet these eligibility criteria, you can still show him to one or more titles. Mixed-breeds, dogs who have been surgically altered, etc. can earn special titles by competing at fun matches. Write to the mixed-breed organizations listed at the back of this book for details.

Chapter 1

Is Your Dog Ready To Show?

PROOF TRAINING

There are several ways you can judge your dog's readiness to show before investing your $12 to $15 in an entry fee. There are no guarantees, of course, but you can weigh the odds in your favor. Many trainers emphasize "proof-training" for their canine students. Proof-training means exposing the dog to as many possible distractions and strange situations as you can devise. For example, dogs can be proofed on the stay exercises with all kinds of noises, with food and squeaky toys being thrown near them and with other dogs running loose while the dogs retain their positions. Check with your instructor about proofing on other exercises. If you train alone, you will have to be creative and ingenious about arranging for distractions. When you cannot trick your dog into making a mistake in training, it is probably time to move on.

PATTERN TRAINING (RUN-THROUGHS)

Many dogs also benefit—especially in the advanced classes—from pattern training. This means running your dog through all of the exercises in sequence, with no corrections, to assess his strengths and weaknesses. Both the handler's and dog's anxiety levels may decrease when they know what will come next. Some trainers object to pattern training on the grounds that it bores the dog. Ideally, pattern training is interspersed with work on individual exercises or parts of exercises.

Once the dog and hander team is secure in the performance of the individual exercises and of the entire set of exercises, it is time to begin attending matches.

MATCHES

Matches are practice shows. They provide a training ground for dogs, handlers, judges and show-giving clubs. They are also used as fund-raisers for clubs and other organizations. They are not always well organized, partly because the size of the entry is unpredictable. Plan to be there most of the day, especially if you are entering the Novice class. Matches provide a handler with the opportunity to learn some things about his dog. Some behaviors with which you might want to experiment are:

1) How much warm-up time does my dog need to be sharp in the ring?
2) When I am warming my dog up, will he resent or be crushed by a correction, or does he need a few pointed reminders of what I expect in the ring?
3) Does my dog work better if he is isolated for an hour? several hours?
4) Does he need to be crated or in the car (if it is not too hot) or does he work better if kept on a down-stay at ringside?
5) Does he require calming down or revving up just before we go in the ring to give his best performance?
6) Does my dog work better if he is fed the morning of the show?
7) Does "foreign" water give my dog diarrhea (if so, prepare to bring sufficient water from home to last all day)?

It is important to maintain your perspective regarding wins or losses at matches. While matches are very competitive in some areas of the country, in many other places they are meant only to provide opportunities for evaluation and correction. Wins at matches have no real significance except for non-registerable dogs. Most match judges are sincerely trying to do a good job, but, like you and your dog, they are at the match to learn. Some match judges are inexperienced and ill-informed about the regulations. Their scores are often wildly erratic—either much too high or much too low. They have been known to invent their own versions of the regulations. Any advice such judges offer the beginning handler should be verified with someone whose reliability and accuracy the handler is sure of. In most areas of the country, dogs who have completed their titles should not be entered in those same level classes competitively. That is, a dog who has earned his C.D. should be entered in the Novice class "For Exhibition Only" and should not be eligible for any prizes or awards. It is often useful to enter an advanced dog in the Novice class to polish heeling or deal with loss of confidence. It is also generally acceptable to show a dog for exhibition only if you wish to run him through the

Open or Utility classes with the jumps set lower than would be required at an AKC trial. Furthermore, if you know in advance that your dog will need a double command or a correction on a particular exercise, it is appropriate to so advise the judge. The judge will generally permit this assistance, but should automatically fail the dog for the exercise. That's fine—the point of going to the match was not necessarily to qualify, but rather to make the dog understand that he must perform the exercises in the way you require.

There are two types of matches: sanctioned matches and non-sanctioned matches (also called "fun" or "correction" matches). These may be open to all breeds or may be limited to only certain breeds. They may involve either conformation or obedience or both.

Sanctioned Matches

Sanctioned matches are run like AKC shows. They are limited to purebred dogs of recognized breeds and no physical correction is permitted in the obedience rings. Dogs may receive verbal correction, and, at the discretion of the judge, exercises may be repeated. Sanctioned matches are held by clubs attempting to meet AKC requirements for holding regular shows and obedience trials. They also serve as a training ground for new judges, who are required to officiate at a certain number of such matches to be eligible to judge at AKC obedience trials. Non-regular classes (other than Novice, Open, and Utility) may be offered, according to the needs of the area. Some sanctioned matches require pre-entry and some are restricted to dogs who have only earned certain titles (for example, no dog who has earned a U.D. may compete). The advertising flyers should provide this information.

Fun Matches

Fun matches may be organized in a number of different ways. There may be separate rings for the group exercises and non-regular classes such as sub-novice, graduate novice, brace, or just-for-fun classes such as mixed-braces (Newfoundlands and Papillons, e.g.) or trade-handler classes may be offered. Reasonable physical correction is permitted. Some people find it useful to enter the dog twice, either in the same class or in both the "A" and "B" sections of the class. The first time through, no corrections are given so that the dog's level of performance can be assessed. The second time through, corrections or help can be given to ease the dog over the rough spots or to prevent repetition of mistakes. When your dog has performed to your satisfaction at several matches and has shown himself capable of qualifying with some degree of consistency, it is probably time to enter him in a licensed obedience trial.

FINAL THOUGHTS ON READINESS

Unless you live in an area where there are very few shows available, it is beneficial to both dog and handler to wait until they are reasonably confident before entering an AKC trial. Be aware, however, that readiness varies based on the dog's individual character and on the class entered. Many dogs can become so steady on the Novice exercises that they have a 90-95 percent likelihood of qualifying. Somewhat fewer dogs can reach that level of steadiness when they begin showing in Open (although many achieve it while showing in Open B). Utility is another matter. Because of the complexity of the behaviors required of the dog, very few dogs reach those high levels of reliability. The dog's understanding of the exercises seems to come and go without warning ("the fall-aparts"), even when they have been trained and shown in this class for long periods of time. It seems that luck has a powerful hand in determining the percentage of qualifying scores in the Utility class.

Chapter 2

Entering A Licensed Trial

JUDGING THE JUDGE

It is advisable to find out who will be judging the class you intend to enter. Many judges run training classes, but their students may not show under them. This does not apply to a judge who puts on a brief training clinic in your area, but rather to the judge whose classes you attend on a regular basis. If you stop attending classes run by a judge, you must wait a year before showing your dog under him or her.

As you attend matches and trials, you will begin to hear stories—occasionally tales of horror—about various judges. You would do well to investigate further before giving credence to such rumors. There are certainly incompetent, capricious and unpleasant obedience judges loose in the community, and you may indeed wish to avoid entering classes over which they are officiating. However, one disgruntled exhibitor does not a bad judge make. If you hear a negative story about a particular judge, ask several experienced people to verify it. Remember, judges have bad days and they make mistakes like anyone else. Furthermore, some exhibitors have an inflated opinion of their dog's ability and may resent the truly observant judge who catches every error and scores dog and handler accordingly. If several different people have confirmed a particular judge's incompetence or unpleasant behavior, you may be wise to consider entering a different class (see page 13) or passing up that particular trial.

THE TRIAL SITE

It is also advisable to try to secure some information about the trial site before sending in your entry. Will obedience be held indoors

9

or outdoors? (Be aware that some indoor all-breed shows designate certain classes to be held outdoors.) If your dog has only been trained outdoors, you would do well to expose him to walking on rubber mats before entering an indoor trial. Some trial sites locate the obedience rings near the building entrance or near the snack bar. If your dog is somewhat shy, or has special problems with distractability, these trials may be more than he can handle. You should also try to learn about the type of surface on which you will be working. Some trials are held on loose dirt (in horse barns, for example) which is hard for short-legged dogs to handle. There are outdoor trials held on hot asphalt, which is especially painful for dogs without much coat. Ask your instructor or a more experienced exhibitor for information. You can also contact the trial-giving club and ask questions about the site (the club secretary's address will appear in the Premium List).

HANDICAPPED HANDLERS

Physically disabled exhibitors are welcome to compete at AKC obedience trials if they can get around the ring without the assistance of another person. Judges or stewards will guide visually impaired persons between exercises. Deaf people who have difficulty with oral communication might want to bring along an interpreter who will not be allowed to enter the ring with the deaf person, but who can assist the exhibitor in establishing some system of signals to be used by the judge. Disabled exhibitors' dogs must perform all parts of every exercise, but judges are usually most helpful in accommodating to the disability. There have been some outstanding dogs trained and handled by wheelchair-bound exhibitors who have competed success-fully with able-bodied handlers. It is, of course, absolutely vital that people with mobility limitations investigate both the accessibility of the trial site and the floor surface of the obedience rings. Even if you can bring your wheelchair into the building, you are not likely to do well if the ring surface is loose dirt or damp tanbark.

FILLING OUT THE ENTRY FORM

You must use an official AKC entry form to enter an AKC trial. These forms are included in the Premium List which is published at least a month before the date of the show. The Premium List tells the exhibitor who is judging, which classes are offered, which trophies and prizes (if any) are offered, gives the name and address of the show site and directions to it. You can obtain Premium Lists from the organizations which put on dog shows (known as show superintend-ents), or by writing to the trial-giving club (whose address can be

FLATIRONS KENNEL CLUB, INC.

Boulder County Fairgrounds   95th & Nelson Road   Longmont, Colorado

SATURDAY, MAY 26, 1984

ENTRY FEE (including 50 cent AKC recording fee) is $12.00 for the first entry of each dog except Puppy, Novice (Breed) & Bred-by-Exhibitor Classes which are $8.00. Each additional entry of the same dog is $8.00. When a dog is entered in more than one class, the highest priced class is considered the first entry. Junior Showmanship Competition is $4.00. Veteran Classes are $12.00.

ENTRIES CLOSE WEDNESDAY NOON, MAY 9, 1984 at Superintendents Office.

MAIL ENTRIES with Fees Payable to JACK ONOFRIO, SUPERINTENDENT, Post Office Box 25764, Oklahoma City, Oklahoma 73125.

NOTICE: PLEASE PUT BREED & NAME OF SHOW ON CHECK.   I ENCLOSE $ 12 .....for entry fees

	OFFICE USE ONLY	SC		Bd		S
CL 1	CL 2	OB 1	OB 2	JS		O

IMPORTANT — Read carefully instructions on Reverse Side Before Filling Out. Numbers in the boxes indicate sections of the instructions relevant to the information needed in that box. (PLEASE PRINT)

BREED Belgian Tervuren	VARIETY [1]	SEX Dog

DOG [2] [3] SHOW CLASS	CLASS [3] DIVISION Weight color etc

ADDITIONAL CLASSES	OBEDIENCE TRIAL CLASS Novice A	JR SHOWMANSHIP CLASS

NAME OF (See Back) JUNIOR HANDLER (if any)

FULL NAME OF DOG   Ch. Fern Hill Act One

X AKC REG NO Enter number here WD365671	DATE OF BIRTH 04-12-76
□ AKC LITTER NO	
□ I L P NO	PLACE OF [X] U S A □ Canada □ Foreign
□ FOREIGN REG NO & COUNTRY	BIRTH Do not print the above in catalog

BREEDER   Barbara S. Handler

SIRE   Ch. Icarus de Sharrvonne C.D.

DAM   Ch. Xquisite de Braise Rouge U.D. T.

ACTUAL OWNER(S)   Barbara S. Handler
(PLEASE PRINT)
OWNER'S ADDRESS   100 Any Road

CITY Anytown   STATE CO   ZIP 80000

NAME OF OWNER'S AGENT (IF ANY) AT THE SHOW   CODE I

I CERTIFY that I am the actual owner of the dog, or that I am the duly authorized agent of the actual owner whose name I have entered above. In consideration of the acceptance of this entry. I (we) agree to abide by the rules and regulations of The American Kennel Club in effect at the time of this show or obedience trial, and by any additional rules and regulations appearing in the premium list for this show or obedience trial or both, and further agree to be bound by the "Agreement" printed on the reverse side of this entry form. I (we) certify and represent that the dog entered is not a hazard to persons or other dogs. This entry is submitted for acceptance on the foregoing representations and agreement.

SIGNATURE of owner or his agent duly authorized to make this entry   TELEPHONE I 666-666-6666

Page 17

A sample entry form. Be sure to sign the form, indicate the correct division as well as class, and include the entry fee.

obtained by writing to the AKC). A list of dog show superintendents can be found at the back of this book. Trial dates and locations are listed regularly in "*Pure Bred Dogs, American Kennel Gazette*" (known to its intimates as "*The Gazette*"). This monthly magazine is frequently available at your local public library or you can subscribe to it by writing to the AKC at the address provided in the introduction. If you attend several shows or trials put on by the same dog show organization, they will put your name on their mailing list and you will receive premium lists for all of the local shows and trials which use the services of that superintendent. You can also telephone the office of the superintendent for information about the trial site, entry fees, closing date, etc. Many obedience clubs do not use the services of a show superintendent, so you must contact the club directly to obtain its premium list. You can use an entry blank from any official premium list to enter a different trial. Simply cross out the pre-printed name, location and date and write in the information for the trial you wish to enter. If you are unsure of the entry fee, you might want to send a check for a few dollars more than the average entry fee in your area. The excess will be refunded to you by mail or at the show.

Be certain to fill out all of the spaces on the entry form, and copy the information exactly as it appears on your dog's AKC registration slip. A sample entry form can be found on page   . Study it carefully before filling out your first entry form. Be certain the form is legible; typing the information is ideal. You may use a pre-printed return address label (the kind you buy to use on your letters) in the section marked "Actual Owner(s)." If your name and address are not readable, you may not get the judging schedule and your entry information back before the day of the trial.

WHICH CLASS - "A" or "B"?

Certain classes are restricted to certain dogs and handlers. Here is a list of the classes and the rules for entering each.

Novice A - For the new exhibitor with his first dog. You may only show a dog you own or co-own, or which is owned by a member of your immediate family. *Beware: if you (a new exhibitor) co-own a dog with another person, and that person has put even **one** obedience title on any other dog, the dog you co-own is ineligible for Novice A—even if the co-owner has never trained the dog in question.* The AKC has no way of knowing who trained the dog. You may show only one dog in Novice A; any subsequent dogs you train must be shown in Novice B. If you have trained two dogs simultaneously, you may only enter one in Novice A (if he is eligible), but you may enter the other in Novice B.

Novice B - For all other novice dogs, including those you are training for another person.

Open A - For dogs who have confirmed Companion Dog (CD) titles, handled by their owners, co-owners or their immediate families. Many people misunderstand Open A: unlike Novice A, *you may show as many dogs as you like in this class, as long as you are the owner or co-owner of record.*

Open B - Once your dog's Companion Dog Excellent (CDX) title has been confirmed, you may continue to show him indefinitely in Open B. In addition, Open B is the class for open dogs not owned by their handlers and for all open dogs owned or co-owned by judges.

Utility A - Has the same restrictions as Open A. The dogs must be owner-handled and must not have confirmed U.D. titles.

Utility B - Is the counterpart to Open B. Most clubs do not split Utility into A and B sections, but rather offer one Utility class for both finished dogs and those still struggling toward their titles.

In general, the competition for high scores and class placements is less keen in the ''A'' classes than in the ''B'' classes. The handling is less polished, and the dogs are not usually as steady. This can be important if you have a dog with stay problems who is easily lured out of position by other dogs' misbehaving. The group exercises in the ''B'' classes are usually—not always—less chaotic. If your dog is ineligible for ''A'' classes because of ownership, or if the judge is one under whom you have already earned a qualifying score, you may always choose to enter the ''B'' class; it is unrestricted. If you mistakenly show your dog in an ''A'' class when it is ineligible, the AKC will eventually discover the error (it may take several months) and will notify you that the dog's title, if any, is rescinded and all awards made to your dog are cancelled. Any ribbons and trophies must be returned to the clubs who awarded them, and you must start all over in the correct class.

About seven to ten days before the show or trial, you will receive a judging schedule or program in the mail. This will give you the time that your class begins, the number of dogs entered in each class, and the number of the ring in which your class will be held. There will also be either a copy of your entry form with your armband number written in, or a printed card (an entry ticket) listing your dog's name and your assigned armband number. This ticket may also be used as an admission pass to the hall or fairgrounds where the trial will be held. Given this information, you can calculate approximately what time you will show. For example, the schedule might say, ''Novice A - 8:00 a.m. - #'s 020-075.'' If your armband number is 037, you will be the 17th exhibitor in a class of 55 dogs. Classes are generally judged at the following rates: Novice - eight dogs per hour; Open

- seven dogs per hour; Utility - six dogs per hour. Therefore, you would be likely to show a little after 10:00 a.m. However, this is only a rough estimate and should be used with caution. Half the dogs ahead of you may be absent, particularly if the weather is bad or if it is the last trial of several on the same weekend. Also, some judges seem to feel a personal challenge to be finished the fastest and run their rings like some sort of race.

You cannot show a bitch in season in the obedience ring. If your bitch comes in season after the entries have closed, some clubs will refund your entry fee. Check the premium list. If the club is forced to change judges after the entries have closed, you may also request a refund, in writing, before the day of the trial, from the superintendent or trial secretary. Generally, your refund will be mailed to you within a few weeks.

Chapter 3

Trial Day Arrives

LOOKING LIKE A PRO

The way you and your dog look at a trial makes a statement about you. You have put a great deal of time into training your dog. Now, spend an extra hour or two on his grooming to show the world you are proud of him. No matter how far your dog is from the ideal described in the breed standard, you owe it to him to groom him as though he were a breed champion (and if he *is* a breed champion, it is even more important that he be presented looking his best). This means checking that his nails are cut short, his coat is clean and free of mats, and that he is trimmed, if that is appropriate for his breed. Your dog may be the only representative of his breed that the public— or even other exhibitors—sees, and the way he looks will affect their impression of the entire breed. Judges cannot help but be impressed by a smartly groomed dog and handler. This should not affect the dog's score, but your joint appearance sets the tone for your performance in the ring. Furthermore, no judge should have to handle a dirty dog.

Now that the dog is spruced up, it is time to look at the handler. Obedience is not a contact sport, and there is no reason for any handler to appear in the ring in old jeans and a worn-out t-shirt. Show respect for yourself and your dog by dressing nicely. Think about the colors and styles you wear, as they may have an influence on the dog's performance. It is not a bad idea to wear pants and shoes the same color as your dark colored dog. It makes the occasional slightly crooked sit less noticeable. If you are going to use hand-signals in the ring, consider wearing a light-colored shirt and a dark jacket so that your clothing will contrast with your surroundings, giving the dog a better chance of seeing your arm movements. If the building is very dark, you can expose the light-colored garments and vice-versa. Wear comfortable shoes with rubber soles. Noisy boots or wooden clogs can make enough noise to be construed as an additional signal to the dog on the heeling exercise, causing points to be deducted. A woman who wishes to wear a skirt or dress in the ring should be certain that it does not hit the dog in the face. She should wear a skirt while practicing, as some dogs are not used to seeing material flapping between themselves and the handler. For the same reason it is wise to avoid dangling jewelry, and men should wear tie tacks to keep their ties from flapping at the dog, especially when taking a retrieved article.

Showing small dogs or short-legged dogs requires extra forethought by the handler. Proper footwear is especially important, as feet loom so large to the small dog. Avoid wide-legged pants that will flap in the dog's face and force him out of heel position.

Dottie LaFleur and Keeshond, Zureeg B My Sadie, C.D., demonstrate what not to wear in the obedience ring. Note the floppy pants and incorrect shoes.

While Dottie looks better, she is still inappropriately dressed. Note the shoes and Sadie's annoyed expression.

LEFT: **Here are Kay Green and Basset Hound, Ch. Strathalbyn Apollo
T.D. dressed to win! (Photo by Craig Green)**

EQUIPMENT

The regulations spell out the types of collars and leashes which are acceptable in the obedience ring. Plain, buckled collars, or slip collars of fabric, leather or chain may be used. The regulations forbid, therefore, slip collars which also have a snap or a buckle, or which have more than two rings. Pinch or prong collars are not permitted *on the grounds* of a trial, show or sanctioned match. The collar should fit properly and not be so tight that it makes an indentation in the dog's neck, or so loose that the dog looks as though it could step through the collar at any moment. Owners of small dogs are the worst offenders, often bringing toy dogs into the ring with collars so big that the dogs trip over them. There must not be any tags hanging from the collar. Leashes may be of leather or fabric (not chain or plastic) and must only be long enough to allow for slack in the heel on leash. There is no regulation requiring a six-foot leash. The collar and leash must be separate. I once judged a man with a fluffy-coated Afghan, who surprised me at the end of the Figure 8, by slipping off the entire nylon show-lead, leaving the dog collarless. I sent him out to find a correct collar and leash and finished judging him later. The leash may be hooked to either or both rings of the slip collar.

These collars are *not acceptable.* **The leather collar would be fine if the tags were removed.**

These collars are *acceptable* in the obedience ring.

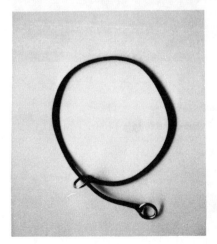

OTHER SUPPLIES

You would do well to make and keep a list of the equipment you need, and check things off as you load the car to go to the trial. Your list is likely to include a dog crate, treats or toys (if you use them), a container of water, a drinking bowl, spare collars and leashes in case one breaks, grooming equipment, a towel or rug for the dog to

A poorly fitted collar on Pembroke Welsh Corgi, Busy-B's Kit Fox, C.D.X., owned by Joanne Peterson.

Now we add a heavy leash with a large snap, and it is a wonder the dog can walk at all.

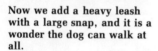

Here she is in a properly fitted buckle collar.

lie on, a folding chair (unavailable at most outdoor trials) and your lunch (the food usually sold at dog shows is notoriously inedible). You may have other items to add to the list, including dumbbells, scent discrimination articles, portable jumps, etc. It is permissible to practice with jumps beyond the trial limits, as will be outlined a bit later. Dog equipment vendors are often present at dog shows (less frequently at separate obedience trials) so you may be able to fill in any gaps at the trial.

If you will be attending an outdoor trial, be aware that bad weather is no reason to stop a dog show. Carry rain gear, including extra towels to keep the dog reasonably dry. You must also keep your dog cool in the heat. Some trial sites have little or no shade. Some people carry extra ice to put in the bottom of the dog's crate. You can turn a metal crate pan upside down and put several blocks of *Blue Ice*® underneath (be careful, however, that the dog cannot reach the *Blue Ice*; it contains poisonous antifreeze). Many exhibitors provide shade for the dogs by covering the tops of exercise pens or crates with sheets, or, preferably with silvered blankets that reflect the sun.

If you are traveling any distance from home, you should include some medical supplies with your equipment. An anti-diarrheal preparation such as *Kaopectate*® or *Pepto Bismol*®, preferably in tablets rather than messy liquid form, is indispensable. If your dog tends to have digestive problems away from home, check with your vet about a more powerful medication which you can carry on trips. Take an adequate supply of any regular medication your dog requires. There is a veterinarian on call at every show or trial. If your dog is injured or becomes ill you can request that the club call the vet. You will be expected to pay for the vet's services in most instances.

AT THE TRIAL

It is generally a good idea to arrive at least two hours before your dog is scheduled to show. This allows time for you to get lost on the way, find the parking area, unload your paraphernalia and find your ring, while still giving the dog time to settle. By attending matches, you have learned how much settling time your dog requires to do his best in the ring. Take this into account when planning your arrival time. The class cannot begin before the published time, but judges do not have to permit latecomers to exhibit. If you are unavoidably late (a flat tire or other real disaster), apologize to the judge and stewards and inquire if you have been marked absent. If not, the judge will tell you when you may show, often at the end of the class.

At a large, all-breed show, it is easy to become confused on the show grounds. Obedience rings are usually clustered together, and are often separated from the breed rings. If the rings are not numbered consecutively, look for the rings with the jumps.

Soon after you arrive, it is a good idea to buy a catalogue. This is a small book listing the names and addresses of all the exhibitors as well as the dogs' registered names. You will find the obedience listings at the back of the catalogue. Obedience dogs are generally shown in the order in which their names are printed ("catalogue order"). If you have a problem with showing in catalogue order, such as a conflict with another ring, you must approach the judge well before your scheduled time to show (preferably before the class begins) and request to show earlier or later. The judge is *not* required to permit this but most are accommodating if the request is polite and reasonable. Similarly, if you are showing two dogs in the same class, the judge may permit you to put them in different stay groups if you do not have an extra handler. Again, *this is the judge's choice, not his obligation.*

Check to see that your name is listed in the correct class. If your name does not appear, or if it is listed in an incorrect class, take your entry ticket to the show superintendent who will have a large table in some prominent place, or to the trial secretary, and ask that the problem be corrected.

If everything is in order, look at the front of the obedience listings and read about the various trophies or prizes being offered. There may be a prize offered for the highest scoring dog of a breed, or of a group, for which you are eligible. In some cases, you must register for certain prizes at the trophy table or at your ring. These include trophies for people living in a certain geographical area, junior handlers (under 18), senior handlers (over 50 or 55), etc.

SPORTSMANSHIP

Now that you and your dog are on the trial grounds, there are some things you should and should not do. The AKC requires all exhibitors to conduct themselves in a sportsmanlike manner, and backs up that expectation by giving show-giving clubs the power to suspend exhibitors' privileges for periods of time from one month to one year, or more. Sportsmanship in this case implies courtesy to judges, to competing exhibitors and gentle treatment of the dog. Here are some specific areas to consider.

Corrections - You may not train or practice with your dog anywhere within the show or trial limits, which are supposed to be clearly marked. This means no collar corrections, no hand or foot corrections and no excessive verbal discipline is permitted. Your dog must be on leash at all times except when he is in the ring. Commands you would normally use to walk your dog around the trial grounds are permitted. While it is not forbidden for you to do some training beyond the show or trial limits, this does not mean that you can go across the road or into the parking lot and brutalize your dog. Corrections on the trial grounds were forbidden some years ago because some exhibitors were becoming abusive, and because even moderate corrections can appear abusive to spectators. If your dog requires harsh correction in order to behave in the ring, perhaps you are showing him prematurely and need to spend some more time training him. A warm-up with your dog at ringside should be limited to a few steps of heeling or a few turns with no corrections, or a few moments of play with a favorite toy (if this does not disturb other exhibitors) or a few quick treats. Of course, any warm-up within the trial limits must be done with the dog on leash.

Controlling Your Dog - Before you sign an entry form for an AKC show or obedience trial, read the agreement on the back. Among other things, it says that the exhibitor is responsible for any damage done by his dog. This means that you are liable for your dog's behavior. It is your legal and ethical responsibility to prevent your dog from being a nuisance or a danger to other dogs and to their exhibitors. If you know your dog has a tendency to look for trouble, don't show him until you are sure he will not be the one to start a fight. It is bad enough when a dog who is normally peaceful becomes aggressive at a trial (generally in a response to the pressure of so many bodies in a limited area, or to the handler's tension), but to take a dog you know you cannot control off leash into a show situation is inexcusable. If your dog attacks another dog, you must pull him off (speak to your instructor about ways to break up dog fights) and you should offer to assist the exhibitor of the other dog if veterinary attention is needed. You must accept financial responsibility for any injuries your dog causes to canines or to humans who are trying to separate combatant dogs. If your dog attacks a person, the same rules apply. If it occurs in the ring, the dog will be disqualified (see page 28), even if the person he attacks is his own handler. Again, it is *absolutely inexcusable* for someone to take a known vicious dog to an obedience trial.

EXERCISING YOUR DOG

This phrase has nothing to do with calisthenics, but rather refers to elimination of body wastes. It is important that your dog empty his bowels and bladder before he enters the ring. If he relieves himself at any time while in the ring for judging, he will not receive a qualifying score. Some dogs have the frustrating habit of being unwilling to eliminate in a strange place. Try to find a surface similar to what he has at home, but respect any off-limits signs on the show or trial grounds. More and more show sites are being closed to dog shows because exhibitors are inconsiderate and permit their dogs to eliminate wherever they choose to, ruining floors, lawns, etc. Clubs must provide exercise areas for dogs. At indoor trials, these are generally covered with saw-dust and clean-up equipment is usually nearby. (At some larger all-breed shows, clean-up crews are hired to keep the grounds and pens clean.) If you must exercise your dog outside the designated area—or if he chooses to exercise himself—find the clean-up equipment or a member of the cleaning crew and see that the offending matter is removed immediately. Do not look the other way and pretend it wasn't your dog who made that mess. If your dog has not had a bowel movement before you take him into the ring, you may want to help nature along by inserting the business end of an unlit paper match into his rectum to stimulate some action. A baby suppository will have the same effect. If you groom your dog at the trial, you must also be considerate of others by picking up any hairballs and confining powders or sprays to a small area.

ENFORCEMENT

The enforcement of the rules regarding sportsmanship rest in two areas. Behavior in the ring is handled by the judge. He or she can and will dismiss, excuse or expel any handler who does not adhere to the spirit and letter of the Regulations. If an exhibitor willfully interferes with the performance of a competitor's dog, or if the judge suspects any cheating (such as carrying food in the ring, giving surreptitious corrections, having another person outside the ring signalling corrections to the dog, etc.) the judge will generally fail the dog. The dog can be shown the next day, hopefully in a more ethical fashion. If, however, a judge believes that a dog has been abused in the ring or on the trial grounds, or if the handler treats the judge in a discourteous manner (arguing about scores, maligning the judge's character, refusing to accept or throwing down a ribbon, standing at ringside making audible negative comments, etc.) the judge will refer the matter to the Obedience Trial Committee of the show-giving club. A fellow exhibitor can also lodge a complaint, especially if there were witnesses to the unsportsmanlike behavior. The Committee will hold a hearing immediately (before the trial is over, if possible), and the exhibitor will have the opportunity to defend himself. The Committee will make a decision on the spot. If the Committee feels the individual's behavior was prejudicial to the good of the sport, it will suspend the handler from exhibiting. This means that any dogs owned or co-owned by that exhibitor cannot be shown until the suspension is lifted, nor can the exhibitor handle a dog in the obedience or conformation ring. The exhibitor can appeal the decision to the Board of Directors of the AKC, or may request reinstatement of his privileges. The AKC, not the Committee, determines the length of the suspension. It may run from one month to an indefinite period.

THE REP

The AKC maintains a staff of field representatives who attend larger shows all over the country. Each of these individuals, known universally as "The Rep," covers shows and trials in a particular geographic area. At a show or trial, the Rep functions as a trained observer, a knowledgeable resource person and a mediator. The Rep does *not* make decisions about problems at a show; that is the job of the show or trial committee. The Rep is a good source of information about rules and regulations, but the power of enforcement still rests with the trial committee.

FINAL CONSIDERATIONS

Now that you have checked the catalogue, exercised your dog and found your ring, there are a few more things to think about before you enter the ring. If your class has started or is about to begin, take your entry ticket to the table at the ring entrance and ask for your armband (remember, the number assigned to you is on your entry ticket). Put the armband on your left arm, turned so that you can look down and see the number (upside down to you). This means it will also be visible to the judge. Now, find a spot to settle yourself and your dog (if he is not crated somewhere else). Do not sit right next to the ring, as this may be distracting to a dog working in the ring. Furthermore, an occasional dog will decide that the spot you had chosen right next to the ring is safe territory, and will leave the ring if he becomes confused (or is feeling naughty) and head back to that spot. If there are rows of chairs, try to sit in the second row.

Spend a few minutes watching what is going on in the ring. Judges are required to standardize their heeling patterns as much as possible, so you and your dog will follow the same pattern of turns, starts and stops as the previous teams. You are likely to be nervous (to put it mildly) and it is helpful to have a mental picture of the pattern so that you will know which way to turn. Some judges employ unusual heeling patterns with unexpected twists such as a "forward-fast" or a "slow-halt." It may be a good idea to practice a few of these odd sequences in your outside-the-trial-limits warm-up (with no rough corrections, however). Watching the pattern will also help you move smoothly from exercise to exercise, as you will know where in the ring each one starts. If you are the first team in the ring, the judge may choose to describe the pattern to you. It is also permissible to ask, but the judge is not required to tell you.

Chapter 4

In The Novice Ring

WHAT TO EXPECT FROM THE JUDGE

It is the judge's responsibility to give you a courteous, thorough, unbiased, knowledgeable assessment of your dog's performance. He or she is also responsible for seeing that the ring conditions meet AKC specifications, especially regarding safe footing for dog and handler. This is more important in the advanced classes where the dog is required to jump. Some judges are warm and friendly; some are brisk and businesslike. You can obtain more information about what the AKC expects of its obedience judges from the booklet, *Guidelines to Obedience Judging*, available free upon written request. The judge has complete control of his ring. His decisions are final and are not subject to discussion (see page 24). You, in turn, are expected to be courteous to the judge (at matches, too).

HANDLING ERRORS

Because obedience competition is an artificial situation—as opposed to, say, taking your dog for a walk in the park—there are rules governing how the exhibitor is expected to perform, in addition to those which apply to the dog. You and your dog are a team, and must work together (re-read the Statement of Purpose at the beginning of this book). Just as the dog will lose points or fail to qualify because he makes a mistake, the same fate awaits you if you err. The judge can and will fail the dog if the handler makes certain errors.

If your failure to qualify is not obvious, the judge will generally tell you about it before you leave the ring. He *must* inform every exhibitor if his dog has qualified or not at the end of the group exercises.

Be aware that your dog may pass all of the individual exercises, and still fail to qualify because he did not earn a total score of at least 170 points. This is known as "failing on points" and happens more often than you might imagine. After I have described the handling requirements for each exercise, I will briefly discuss the criteria for passing or failing so that you can form an accurate image of a qualifying performance.

Non-qualification Vs. Disqualification

Many exhibitors use these terms interchangeably. A non-qualifying score (or NQ, flunk, bust, etc.) simply means that your dog failed to pass in one class at one show. You and the dog can go home, work on the problem exercise and show again at the next trial. A disqualification, however, is a much more serious matter. A dog who is disqualified may not again compete at an AKC event unless and until the owner appeals the disqualification to the AKC and is notified by them that the dog has been reinstated. There are four reasons why a dog would be disqualified: if it is blind, if it is deaf, if it has been artificially altered (see page 2), or if it attacks any person in the ring. Now that you know the difference, you can use the correct terminology and impress your fellow exhibitors with your expertise.

Hands Off

Once you enter the Novice ring, you may not touch your dog except to pet it between exercises. You may guide the dog gently by the collar between exercises, but you may not—under any circumstances, position him with your hands, knees or feet. If you teach your dog to pay attention on command ("watch-me"), you may not touch the dog's head or muzzle when you tell him to look at you.

You are allowed to give only one command (or command and signal, if permitted) in most circumstances. If you correct your dog verbally in the ring you will fail the exercise. If you move toward the dog to correct him, you will be excused and will not be permitted to complete the exercises. If your dog is very excited when you enter the ring, or between exercises, and refuses to sit at heel and if you have told him to sit several times without success, look at the judge to see if he or she is going to tell you what to do. If not, you may choose to sit him gently with your hands and take the deduction for a handling error. After the judge has said, "Exercise finished," many people will tell their dog to sit straight if their dog's position at the end of the exercise is not perfect. Not only do some judges consider this to be training in the ring and deduct points accordingly, but it is also of questionable value to telegraph to the judge that your dog sat crooked, as the judge may not have thought that was the case. Sour looks at the dog while it is heeling, sitting in front or finishing can be equally detrimental to your score.

The Heel On Leash and Figure 8

When your number is called, you will enter the ring with your dog on a loose leash. Be sure to empty your pockets of any food treats and toys and leave them at your seat or (if the judge does not object), on the table at the ring entrance. Proceed to the spot where all of the other teams started and have your dog sitting quietly in the heel position. The judge will ask if you are ready, and it is permissible to call for the dog's attention before saying that you are (but remember not to touch him). It is a good idea to get in the habit of giving the same response every time the judge asks if you are ready (for example, replying, "Yes" or "Ready"). This is an extra, legal reminder to the dog that the action is about to start. Many handlers nod their heads in response, but a verbal response is clearer to the judge. Some handlers are so paralyzed with fear that they stand and let their eyes glaze over as a response to, "Are you ready?" This is rather frustrating to the judge and makes a poor impression.

Your commands to the dog may be in any language and you may substitute a hand signal for any command. You may not use the dog's name with a hand signal, except on those exercises in which you are permitted to use the name, verbal command and signal. You are not required to use the dog's name before a command. If your dog tends to anticipate commands, you may want to consider this option. When you do use both name and command they must be spoken with no pause between them: "Fido, Sit". Not, "Fido . . . . . . Sit." Pausing between name and command is a handling error. Commands must be given in a normal tone of voice. Loud commands will be penalized.

If your dog is lame or becomes ill (vomits, e.g.) in the ring, the judge will excuse you. This means you do not have to complete the exercises or return for the group exercises. (Obviously, if your dog is ill, you should take him home and/or seek medical attention.) If your dog begins to urinate or have a bowel movement in the ring, attempt to move him off the mat, if any, and then let him finish. Dragging the dog out of the ring merely extends the area of disaster. Be aware that the dog will fail to qualify, but generally will be permitted to complete the exercises. The steward or clean-up crew will remove the debris.

The way you walk will affect your dog's performance and therefore your score on the heeling exercises. Your pace should be brisk enough that the dog must move at a trot. Walking too slowly can be considered as adapting your pace to that of the dog, resulting in points deducted for a handling error. Heeling is an exercise in which the dog accompanies you—not the other way around. You set the pace for the team. You should also attempt to be consistent in all of your movements so the dog will know what to expect. Your instructor will show you how to make good turns, so that your footwork is an asset—not a liability—to your dog. If you train alone, consult one of the many books available or try to attend a training clinic in your area. You must also practice walking in a straight line. This is easier to do when walking on mats. If your dog is heeling wide (too far to your left), you must not move to the left to make him look better. This is a handling error and will result in points being lost. Similarly, do not move to the right to avoid a dog who is crowding you. Once you are in the ring, it is too late to correct these errors. Let the dog make the mistakes. Your attempts to compensate will be noticed by most judges, and they will likely be annoyed by your trying to fool them. Be sure to keep the dog on the mat; you walk on the slippery floor in your non-skid shoes.

People with small or short-legged dogs must be especially conscious of their footwork. It is important that they refrain from letting their feet drift in front of the dog and that they do not kick up their heels in the dog's face when doing the fast, as this will cause the dog to lag or swing wide.

When the judge calls for a slow pace, you must make a noticeable change in your speed. Most trainers advise long, slow, even steps, rather than tiny, mincing ones. When the fast is called, you must run. It is not true that your dog must break into a gallop, as long as he stays in heel position. You are permitted to take several steps to change from one pace to another and back again. Abrupt changes of pace make for a jerky-looking heeling performance.

Similarly, you may take two or three steps to halt after the command is given (but not five or six steps). You must stop in a straight line, without stepping to your right or left to make the dog's sit appear straighter. Once you have stopped, do not shuffle your feet forward or backward. If your dog fails to sit, do not correct him verbally or physically. He will lose several points, but will not fail the exercise. If your dog swings around and sits in front of you, or goes all the way around you, wait until the judge again says, "Forward," and then gently guide the dog into heel position with the leash and walk on.

When making left and right turns, do not round the corners. Make a square turn, without pausing, but not in military fashion. Do not pause on the about turns, as this will be considered an illegal aid to the dog. Also, be careful not to back into the about turns as this is another way of accommodating to the dog. Have your instructor or a friend observe your footwork with these factors in mind. It is easy to get into bad habits while training, habits which will cost unnecessary deductions from your score. A final word on footwork: while it is helpful to the dog when the handler moves in a consistent manner, the AKC does not require any specific footwork. You will not lose points for starting to walk with the right foot, although handlers are traditionally taught to start with the left foot. Inexperienced match judges are notorious for mistakenly deducting points for this.

If your dog is not sitting straight when the judge asks if you are ready to begin the heeling pattern, you may tell him to straighten himself. Many handlers, become obsessed with this initial step and circle around and around attempting to get the dog into the desired position. This is both very time consuming and very annoying to the judge, who has a limited amount of time allotted to judge each dog. If the exhibitor repeats this action enough times, the judge may begin to deduct points for the dog's lack of response to command. If it is consistent with your training program, it may be advisable to teach your dog to straighten himself on command without any circling. Under any circumstances, if the dog does not respond after one or two commands, forget about it and tell the judge you are ready. Remember, judging does not begin until you say you are ready, except when the dog is obviously refusing to respond to commands.

The leash may be held in either hand or in both hands. There should be enough slack in the leash to show that the dog is maintaining heel position of his own free will, but the leash should not hang down so that the dog is likely to trip over it. If the dog lags or forges, do not let out more of the leash in the hopes that the judge will not notice that the dog is not in heel position. Again, let the dog make the mistake, if any. The position of your hands should be one that is comfortable for you and one which looks natural. A good rule of thumb is, would this be a likely hand position for a person walking his well-mannered dog along the street? It not, you may be penalized for a handler error. Whatever hand position you choose, do not change it during the course of the heeling exercise. Exhibitors lose many points by moving their hands during the heeling exercise, especially on the halts. In some cases, this is a result of poor training. The dog has learned to wait for a slight tightening of the leash as a signal to sit, instead of sitting because the handler has stopped walking. It can also be a function of nervousness. Take pains to avoid these movements, whatever the cause. If you are not sure if you are telegraphing subtle correction to the dog with the leash, have somebody observe you.

Do not stare at your dog while you are heeling. This can be counted as a handling error and can also make the dog lag, as he anticipates a correction. You may watch the dog out of the corner of your

Kay Green and Basset Hound Strathalbyn Last Call T.D., demonstrating correct heel position.

Mary Quaco and Gordon Setter, Ch. McO Bedazzle, C.D.X., demonstrating correct handler position while performing the heel free.

eye. Remember, if he is not in heel position, it is too late to do anything about it once you are in the ring. Try to maintain a pleasant facial expression rather than glaring at the dog. This is supposed to be *fun*, after all.

You must not anticipate turns or changes of pace. Wait for the judge to give the order. It is easy to anticipate commands, especially if the ring is small or the judge is slow to give commands. If the judge runs you into a wall, stop and wait for further instructions. Many instructors have their trainees practice sits directly in front of a wall or barrier as preparation for such an occurrence.

Figure 8

After you have praised the dog for completing the heeling pattern, move to the spot where the Figure 8 will take place. Face the judge, standing squarely equidistant from the two posts, and two to three feet back from them. You may start in either direction. Unless your dog crowds badly, you may want to start to your left. Starting to the right often encourages the dog to lag. Check with your instructor. In the Figure 8, the dog must change pace as the handler moves around the posts: faster on the outside and slower on the inside. It is important that you maintain a steady brisk pace, so that the dog adapts to you - not you to him. Keep your circles around the posts even. Do not make a wide circle when the dog is on the inside to avoid being crowded. If your dog lags when he is on the outside circle, do not let the leash out, hoping the judge will not notice that the dog is out of heel position. The judge will not be fooled.

When the Figure 8 is completed, surrender your lead to the steward and move to the spot where the stand for examination will take place. Remember, from now on you may gently guide the dog—by the collar only—between exercises. Some trainers advise their students to try to avoid guiding the dog physically at all, but rather to rely on voice control. Other trainers suggest that rather than holding the live ring of a slip collar to guide the dog, you put your hand on the chain or fabric of the collar to avoid any hint of correction.

Pass or Fail? - It is difficult to fail the heel on leash, but some dogs manage. Things that would cause the dog to fail include: never being in heel position (either lagging behind or forging ahead); attempting to leave the ring; stopping completely; failing to sit at heel at any time (this last one varies from judge to judge). In addition to the common handling errors noted previously, the handler can lose points, or possibly fail, by continuously jerking on the leash, keeping the leash tight so that the dog is forced to stay in position, or giving extra verbal commands to the dog.

Stand for Examination

This is the only exercise in the Novice class in which you may physically manipulate your dog. It is courteous to stand the dog facing the judge. Some shy dogs, however, are less apt to break if approached by the judge from one side or the other. If you have a shy dog, experiment to see if this is applicable. If so, position your dog accordingly in the ring. (There is no guarantee, of course, that the judge will not move around to examine the dog squarely from the front.) You may take any reasonable amount of time to position the dog. Once the dog is standing comfortably, stand up straight and be sure both hands are off the dog and his collar. Give the stay command and walk directly forward until you are six feet from your dog. Generally, this distance is equal to three normal steps or two large steps. Turn and face the dog and stand quietly until the examination is complete. On the judge's order, return around the dog to your right and be careful to stop in heel position. The dog does not have to sit after this exercise, but can be freed and praised directly from the standing position, depending on the training method used.

The most common handling errors are: holding the dog's head or collar in one hand while giving the stay command, backing away from the dog, going farther than six feet away, or not returning all the way to heel position.

Pass or Fail? - If the dog remained standing where he was left until the examination was completed, he should pass, although he will lose points for moving his feet. A dog who moves away from the place where he was left before or during the exam will not pass. This is a matter of interpretation, but it would be safe to assume that a dog moving one body length from his original position would fail. Judges differ in their opinions. Similarly, judges differ in their interpretations of shyness. The regulations state that a dog who "displays shyness" should receive a score of zero, but does this refer to a dog who leans away from the judge, without ever moving its feet, or to one who moves one foot or two feet? Most judges will not penalize a dog who basically stands his ground. A dog who growls or snaps, however, should always fail. If your dog walks away or sits or lies down after the examination, he will lose points, but should not fail the exercise.

Heel Free

Generally, the heel free will follow the same pattern as the heel on leash and the same rules apply. Again, the position of the handler's hands must be both natural and consistent. It is permissible to hold the left hand at waist level to avoid being bumped by a large dog. You may do this with a small dog as well, but it looks a bit silly. Some

LEFT: Correct heel position as seen from the front. Note Mary's raised left arm.

BELOW: Here Mary double commands her dog by turning her body and attempting to stare the dog into heel position.

handlers hold their right hand at waist level, which also looks rather peculiar and does not seem to serve any purpose.

If your dog stops or leaves heel position, or starts to bolt out of the ring, do not wait for the judge's order, but immediately give a rather firm command to heel (and a signal, as well) and move on. If the dog responds, he will lose some points but may still qualify. Be alert for this and act promptly if it occurs.

Pass or Fail? - The heel free is probably the one exercise in which this determination is most difficult to predict. The exact same performance may cause a dog to fail one day and pass the next. I can only offer you my own criterion as a judge. I will pass a dog who stays in heel position through at least 50% of the pattern. In almost every case, a dog receiving more than one extra command to heel will fail.

The Recall

Following the heel free, move to the position where the recall is to begin. See that your dog is seated squarely on the mat, if any. When the judge orders you to leave, give your command and/or signal to stay and walk briskly away from your dog. Do not creep away, sneaking looks at him over your shoulder, but act as though you believe he is going to wait for your recall command. Turn and face your dog squarely, being careful to allow enough room for him to

Sandy Decker stands correctly as she calls Samoyed, Ch. Trailblazer Winter Dawn, U.D.

finish, and set your feet in the position you will maintain until the exercise is complete. Moving your feet after you have called the dog may be considered a handling error. If you move them after the dog has sat in front of you, you will certainly receive a deduction. *Your hands must hang naturally at your sides.* When you call the dog, use a pleasant tone of voice and smile (you're almost through). Do not make obvious head movements while following the dog's progress as he approaches you. If the dog does not sit in front, and either stands or proceeds directly to heel position, do nothing. If the dog passes you by and heads out of the ring, call him back before he reaches the exit. If your dog fails to come on your command, wait several seconds to see if he is merely reacting slowly. You may then choose to give him a second command. He has already failed the exercise, but should not be allowed to ignore your command. Frequently, in fact, the judge will even order you to give the second command. Do not step toward him to give it. Most judges will permit a second command, but you do run the risk of being excused for training in the ring. Weigh the consequences and decide what to do before you go to a show.

Handlers commonly lose points for using body motions when calling the dog. They bend from the neck or the waist or extend their arms, or even bend their knees while calling the dog. Remember that

**Double Command!
Sandy bends her body
and extends her arms
while calling her dog.**

you must stand with your arms hanging naturally at your sides any time the dog is coming to you.

The finish is not a principal part of any exercise. It can be a source of many lost points, however. The dog may finish to the right or the left. Many exhibitors prefer to teach their dogs to finish in both directions. Then, if the dog sits too far to one side on the sit in front, they can send him to heel position more smoothly. Dogs must move smartly to the heel position, but there is no requirement that the dog jump in the air while finishing. The jump or flip finish is very impressive to watch, and often is fun for the dog, but also provides an extra opportunity for the dog to bump or touch the handler, thereby receiving a deduction. The dog will lose points if he stops to gaze at the spectators or to sniff, or oozes himself slowly into the final sit. Handlers are again prone to attempt to assist the dog—usually unconsiously—by moving their heads, shoulders or knees. Do not follow your dog's progress after giving him the command or signal to finish, but watch out of the corner of your eye for him to appear in heel position. If the dog does not respond to the finish command, wait for the judge to say, "Exercise finished" and then release him. Remember, you are not allowed to train your dog in the ring. If your dog finishes on his own, either by not stopping to sit in front, or by anticipating the command, the judge may or may not give him an additionl "Finish" command. Some judges will do this, even if the dog is sitting perfectly in heel position, to see if the dog will respond to the command.

Pass or Fail? - If the dog waited to be called without moving forward, came on the first command and stopped within an arm's reach he probably passed. If he stood or lay down before he was called, points will be deducted. If he got up and made any movement toward you, before you called him, he probably failed. Points can also be lost if the dog does not come directly to you, stops to sniff or look around, or comes in slowly. The dog who comes in and sits out of reach will also fail. This is a judgment call. According to the regulations, a dog is in reach if it is close enough so that the handler could touch its head without stretching. This is somewhat misleading: if a 6-foot tall man is showing a dachshund, there is no way he could touch the dog's head without stretching. Several years ago a different and somewhat more reasonable criterion appeared in the AKC's *Guidelines for Obedience Judges*. It said that a dog was considered out of reach if an average person could walk between dog and handler without touching either. While this criteria no longer appears in the *Guidelines*, it remains a good rule of thumb.

When the recall exercise is complete, praise your dog and walk toward the ring entrance with the dog under control. Take the leash from the steward or off the table and attach it before you leave the

Kathy Heun stands still while Bernese Mountain Dog, Broken Oaks Gideon V Arjana, does the finish.

Kathy makes a handling error by bending back to watch the dog's progress.

Judy Keller and Staffordshire Bull Terrier, Ch. Barzac's Lady Winifred, C.D., demonstrating a perfect sit in front.

ring. It is courteous to thank the judge for his time. Be sure your attitude is positive, even if the dog failed miserably. The dog does not know that your experience in the ring was negative, but if you telegraph your displeasure to him, you may shake his confidence and affect future performances. If you feel you cannot control your temper (and some very bright dogs appear to delight in testing their handlers by acting totally untrained in the ring), arrange to have a friend take the dog from you as you leave the ring and keep him isolated until you have cooled down.

THE GROUP EXERCISES

The judge will usually advise the stewards as to how many dogs he or she will judge before breaking for a set of group exercises. If there are 12 dogs or less entered in the class, the group exercises will be done at the end. It is important that you keep track of when the break will occur. You would be wise to see that your dog has been exercised and given a drink by the time the last dog in the group is in the ring for the individual exercises. Be sure that your dog is awake and alert as you listen for the stewards to call the dogs in your group to line up in catalogue order. Be courteous enough to be available when this happens; don't be the person who has to be called and called, holding up the entire class. *Remember, unless your dog has been excused, expelled or disqualified, he must do the group exercises even if he has non-qualifed on the individual exercises.* If you have a time conflict with another ring and your dog has already failed, you may ask the judge to excuse you from the group exercises. This is the judge's option, so if he or she does not agree to excuse you, you must appear.

Before group exercises on a hot day at an outdoor show, you may want to wet your dog down to keep him comfortable. Be sure to wet his head, chest and groin thoroughly as these areas will affect his comfort the most.

When you enter the ring with the other dogs, pay attention to the spot where you place your dog. If it is an outdoor trial, look for a flat surface with no burrs, twigs, anthills, etc. At an indoor show, try to avoid placing the dog where two mats are taped together, or where a dog previously fouled the ring. You usually have the leeway to move your dog a few inches to one side of a potential problem area. Remove your armband and leash. Turn to your left (toward the dog) and place them on the ground, several feet behind the dog. Should your dog get up when you turn, you will be between your dog and the next dog in line, so that he is less likely to come nose to nose with his neighbor.

If there is a dog in your group who has broken position and started fights at local matches or previous shows, you may *not* ask to change your order or to be in a different group to avoid the problem dog. You should inform the steward and/or the judge, in a calm and honest manner, of your concern. No judge wants a dog fight in his ring. He will be sure to keep a close eye on the likely offender.

The Long Sit

During this exercise some people go to great lengths to avoid eye contact with their dog, even to the point of appearing a bit odd as they gaze off into space. Others maintain constant eye contact with the dog. Check with your instructor. Either way, you may not attempt to control your dog through any obvious facial contortions or body movements. You are not, however, required to remain motionless. Some exhibitors cross their arms when they are facing their dogs on this exercise as an extra, legal reminder to the dog to remain in place.

Listen to the judge's instructions before you leave your dog. He or she will tell you what to do if your dog breaks position and comes to you or goes to another dog. You may be told to retrieve your dog yourself on the judge's order, or the steward may bring the dog to you to hold. If so, do not correct the dog (tempting though it may be), but tell him to sit and stay in front of you. Do not unthinkingly pet the dog, as this may encourage him to repeat the behavior. The judge may have the steward hold the dog at the side of the ring.

If the dog lies down or stands up as you give him the stay command, you may want to give a verbal command to sit, or even gently reposition him. If he completes the rest of the exercise successfully the judge may give him a qualifying score. This is another individual judgment call. If your dog stands or lies down after you have left him there is nothing you can do about it. Under any circumstances, do not physically correct him when you return. If the dog changes position after you have returned to heel position, he will pass with only a minor point deduction. If, however, you are even one step away from heel position when he breaks, he will fail.

If your dog or the dog next to him rolls over when there is not much space between dogs, you may find that you cannot return to heel position without stepping over one or both dogs. In that case, go around the dog to the right of your dog (as you are facing him). Return around both dogs so that you do not have to step over either dog. If there is no room between your dog and the dog to his left for you to stand next to your dog in the heel position, get as close as you can without stepping over either dog. Ideally, an alert judge will not permit two dogs to roll that close to each other and will remove one or both of them to prevent possible trouble.

You are not required to break your dog from position at the end of the long sit. Some trainers point out that it is not a good idea to excite the dog at the end of the sit and then require him to lie quietly for three minutes. On the other hand, some dogs get in the habit of lying down the moment the long sit is over, in anticipation of the long down. This can become a serious problem when the dog makes his own decision about when the long sit is finished.

The most common handling errors committed on the long sit include the handler physically positioning the dog before the exercise starts, giving loud commands and using body English to make the dog stay, and failing to return all the way to heel position.

Pass or Fail? - If the dog remained in the sitting position from the time you left until you were securely back in heel position without repeatedly barking or whining, he probably passed.

The Long Down

There is no regulation prohibiting or penalizing a repeated command to down, and no dog should lose points for requiring two commands and a hand signal before complying. However, there are times when the dog has clearly decided not to cooperate. If your dog refuses to lie down after you have given him several verbal commands, take hold of his collar and gently put him down. You will lose some points, but will not fail. If your dog lies down at an angle so that he might interfere with another dog, the judge will ask you to reposition him and deduct some points. It is a good idea, therefore, to work with your dog to teach him to lie down directly at your side. Many trainers insist that the dog always assume a particular position for the long down. Ask your instructor about this.

Pass or Fail? - If your dog remained in the down position for the full three minutes, without repeatedly barking or whining, he probably passed. If he stayed down, but crawled or rolled a significant distance from his original spot, he will probably not pass. Remember, when this exercise is finished, the judge will come around and tell you if you have qualified or not.

The End of the Class

If your dog has qualified, take him out for a last exercise break as the class is ending, while the last group exercise is underway. Give him a drink and wake him up with whatever your normal warm-up routine is. No matter how you think your dog performed, wake him up for a potential run-off. You can never predict what a judge may have thought about your performance. If you have tied for a placement in the class, or for a breed trophy; (e.g., highest scoring fuzzy terrier in Novice B), you will be called by armband number to come to the ring for a run-off. This will consist of an off-lead heeling pattern

42

for each dog, individually, generally in catalogue order. The judge may or may not announce the winner on the spot. When the run-offs are complete all of the qualifying dogs will be called back into the ring and scores and placements will be announced. If you and your dog have won first prize in your class, do not leave the show as you may be highest scoring in trial (unless another class has also ended and the winner had a higher score than yours). If there was a trophy listed for which you are eligible, check to see if others are also competing for it. If so, you must wait until every eligible handler's score has been awarded to know if you have won. Trophies (other than class placements) are almost always awarded at the end of the trial after all judging is completed. Occasionally, there are run-offs for these trophies and for Highest Scoring Dog in Trial. These run-offs take place right before final awards are made at the end of the trial or show.

If your dog has done something special—earned his first leg, completed a title, won a special award,—you may want to commemorate the occasion by having a picture taken. The steward can call for the show photographer and you will pose with the judge, the dog and any trophies or ribbons you have won. The photographer will make note of your armband number and send the picture to you through the mail. If you like the picture, you pay for it by return mail. If you are not satisfied, you may return the picture to the photographer by mail.

Get in the habit of going over to the Superintendent's table to check your score before you leave the show grounds. There will be a copy of the judge's book (in which he marked the scores) available for you to see. Be sure that your score was added correctly and that the score listed agrees with the score the judge gave you earlier. If there is a discrepancy, immediately bring it to the attention of the Superintendent. Some exhibitors make a habit of writing down how many points they have lost on each exercise for future reference.

SPECIAL AWARDS

In addition to winning awards at shows, you may also compete for some special awards which are national in scope.

AKC Obedience Degrees - When your dog has qualified in the same class at three shows, under three different judges, the AKC will automatically send you a certificate and publish your dog's name in the "Gazette". You do not have to apply for your certification. If you have not received your certificate within two months of your third qualifying score, contact the AKC Show Records Department by telephone or by mail to verify your qualifying scores. Many people like to earn an extra qualifying score (the security leg) in case an earlier score was somehow lost in the computer records. You may continue to show your dog in either Novice class or in Open A or Utility A until you receive your certificate from the AKC. If you have entered a trial and *the closing date for the entries has passed* when you receive your certificate, you may proceed to show. If the entries have not closed when your certificate arrives, you must withdraw your entry and request a refund of your entry fee.

The "Dog World" Award - "Dog World" magazine will print your dog's name and picture, and send you a certificate, if your dog qualifies for any degree in his first three trials (no failures) with scores of 195 or better. You must write to the magazine to inform them of your eligibility. "Dog World" can be purchased at many news-stands.

THE RATINGS SYSTEMS

The Delaney System - counts the number of dogs your dog has defeated by winning class placements or Highest Scoring Dog in Trial. You earn one point for every dog you defeat. Information is taken from show results published in the "Gazette" and winner's names and dog's names for every breed are published in *Front and Finish,* a monthly national obedience newspaper (P.O. Box 333, Galesburg, Illinois, 61401).

The Shuman System - awards points to dogs who earn qualifying scores in Open and Utility classes (not Novice). The higher the score, the more points are awarded. Results are automatically published in "Front and Finish". Winners are notified in advance that they have placed in the system (but are not told what their ranking is) so that they can send a picture of their dog which will be published along with the listings. Notice that both of these systems recognize dogs by individual breed and by groups, as well as acknowledging the top ten dogs overall. Placing in either of these systems is an honor.

Breed Club Systems - Many national breed clubs also rate dogs of their breed in obedience. They use many different systems and most will publish their results in their national publication and/or notify winners by mail. Some clubs also have travelling trophies which the winner may keep for a year and then pass on to the next winner.

THOUGHTS ON SCORES

Remember that the score you receive is nothing more than one judge's opinion of your dog's performance on a particular day. It has no effect on your dog's affection for you and does not mark your dog as good or bad. It should not affect your relationship with your dog.

Sometimes, however, there are discrepancies you will want to address. If you feel your dog unjustly received a non-qualifying score

The author and her Belgian Tervuren, Ch. & O.T. Ch.
Fern Hill Act One, T.D., have a picture taken with
judge Nancy Pollock to commemorate a victory. (Photo
by Wayne Cott)

or if a judge deducted points for something that makes no sense to you, you may approach the judge and *politely* ask about the score. You may not argue with the judge. It may be that you have misunderstood the regulations pertaining to a particular exercise, or inadvertently made a handling error. Maintain the attitude that you are asking for information and not defending your honor. If the judge has time, he will usually be willing to explain his decision, but he is not required to do so. Remember that judges make mistakes and that scores, once recorded in the judge's book, cannot be changed except to correct computational errors.

If, after discussing the matter calmly, you still feel that the judge was in error or inaccurate or even unfair, there is really nothing you can do about the particular score in question. Judge's decisions are always final. You can, however, take some action to express your dissatisfation. You can speak to the AKC field representative at the show and register a polite complaint. This will not result in your score being changed. A more effective protest would consist of a polite and reasonably worded letter, outlining the situation as you see it, addressed to the Director of the Obedience Department of the AKC, with copies to the show-giving club and to the judge with whom you are in dispute. Do not write a poison-pen letter, but have the courage to bring your charges directly to the people involved. If the judge was truly in error, the AKC will address the issue. If it was a matter of incompetence or deliberate unpleasantness on the part of the judge, and if several people have written similar letters, the club will be unlikely to hire that judge again. Furthermore, word gets around in a given area and the judge will receive fewer and fewer invitations to officiate.

Don't waste too much energy feeling victimized by a score lower than you felt you deserved. These things tend to balance out, and for every low score you get, you will be likely to receive a gift of a higher score than you deserved. These "gift" scores are fun to receive because they are generally unexpected. On one occasion, my Open dog decided that a particular judge was going to do terrible things to him. During the performance, the dog left heel position at least three times (I stopped looking after that). The front sits were all crooked because the dog was watching the judge over his shoulder. The finishes were crooked because the dog was trying to hide behind me. He received a score of 198 and second prize. The next day, the dog gave me one of the very best performances of his career, but received a low score and did not place. The lesson I learned from that weekend was to accept the low scores philosophically and to enjoy the "gift" scores without apologizing to anybody. Keeping your perspective is one of the best lessons the obedience ring can teach you.

A last word before moving on the Open exercises. If you are absolutely certain that a fellow exhibitor has cheated in some way (double handling on group exercises, using food in the ring), it is not up to you to discipline the cheater. You may report the incident to the judge, who may or may not choose to act on your report. If you can prove your accusations or have corroboration from other exhibitors, you can take your concerns to the Obedience Chairman of the club, who can invoke the powers of the Trial Committee as described on page 24. You should do the same thing if you see someone abusing a dog.

Chapter 5

In The Open Ring

Now that you have advanced beyond the Novice level, you will find that there are a few changes in the ring procedures. In the Open and the Utility ring, you may not touch your dog or his collar to correct or guide him. You may still pet him between exercises. You must have voice control of your dog. If you have an exuberant dog be especially careful that he doesn't get too excited between exercises as you will lose points (but will still qualify) if you have to control him physically at any time.

When you check in at your ring, be prepared to report your jump heights to the steward who will mark them in the catalogue. Do not expect the stewards to calculate this for you. If your dog measures on the borderline between two jump heights (that is, if some people measure him at 23¾ " and others measure him right at 24"), there is nothing wrong in reporting the lower heights to the steward. The judge will measure your dog and make his own determination. If you have such a dog, you would do well to practice with him at both possible jump heights. This is especially important if either measurement results in a change in the number of boards used in the broad jump. A 4-board jump looks very different to a dog from a 3-board jump, even though the total distance changed amounts to only four inches.

When you are warming up your dog for the Open Ring there is nothing wrong with setting up jumps beyond the trial limits to practice as long as you give no abusive or rough correction. Some people prefer to have their dogs warm up with stick-jumping instead. Ask your instructor. Even if you do not choose to practice actual jumping, be sure to move your dog around enough to loosen him up before entering the ring, especially if he has been lying down for an hour or more at ringside.

Remember that all of the information regarding handling the dog on the Novice recall applies equally to any exercise in which the dog comes from a distance and sits in front of you. The heel free is the same as in Novice, except that the Figure 8 is also done off leash.

ENTERING THE RING

As you are waiting at the ring entrance for the judge's invitation to come in, look at the jumps and see that they are set correctly. Pay special attention that the correct number of boards is used on the broad jump. Place your leash and dumbbells on the table and stand your dog for measuring. It is acceptable and advisable to hold your dog while he is being measured in case the judge is a bit clumsy with the ruler or the dog has some negative reaction. Many instructors teach the stand for measuring as a regular exercise. If your dog is a bit shy you may try an old professional handler's trick and cover his eyes as the judge approaches with the ruler. This helps some dogs remain calm. If your dog is upset by the measuring process, it is likely to take him a few minutes to recover and will probably have a negative effect on his performance.

THE DROP ON RECALL

One of the choices an exhibitor must make is whether to use a verbal command or a hand signal to down his dog. There are no regulations affecting this choice except that you cannot use both. Many dogs respond better to a signal than to a voice command. On the other hand, a dog has a harder time ignoring a voice command than pretending he did not see a signal. Many dogs manage to ignore both, of course. Check with your instructor and then consider the ring conditions on any particular day. If it is very noisy, a signal may be in order. If the dog is especially distractable, the verbal command may be more compelling. If you do use a hand signal, AKC Regulations permit only two types. You may either extend your hand and arm straight up in the air and then *immediately* drop them to your side, or you may make a circular motion, bringing your extended arm up and around from back to front. In either case, the movement must be continuous with no pause at the top. Such a pause constitutes a double command and will cause you to fail the exercise. Only the arm may move; any bending at the neck or waist will be penalized. Similarly, an excessively loud or nasty command will be penalized. If your dog fails to drop on the first signal or command, you may as well repeat it, knowing you have failed for that day anyway. As long as you do not move toward your dog to correct him, most judges—especially those who are actively training and showing—will not object to the additional command. The worst that can happen is that you will be excused.

Pass or Fail? - The standards are identical to those for the Novice recall. In addition, the dog must not drop before the command or signal is given, and must wait to be called the second time without getting up from the down position. Points are deducted for slow responses to any of these commands.

RETRIEVE ON THE FLAT

The Regulations state that the dumbbell must be proportionate to the size of the dog. This means that the dowel should be long enough to allow the dog to hold it comfortably without pinching his lips. A dowel that is too long encourages the dog to mouth the dumbbell to keep it balanced. A good rule of thumb is to allow one-half inch clearance between the dog's lip and the bell. This means that dogs with long flews (Bassets and most Setters, among others) need a longer dowel than tight-lipped breeds like Dobermans and Spitz-type dogs. Square-faced dogs or those with undershot jaws (such as Pugs, Bostons and Bulldogs) also need longer dowels. The bells should be just tall enough that the dog can pick the dumbbell up without bumping his nose or scraping his underjaw on the ground.

Keeshond, Ch. Maldolph's Baron Von Zureeg, C.D.X., owned by the author and Sue Riegel, holding a correctly fitted dumbbell. Note the ends, painted white for increased visibility.

The bells may be round or square. Most exhibitors find it easier to throw the square-ended dumbbells accurately because they do not roll as badly as the round ones. Check with your instructor. Many exhibitors paint the bells of the dumbbell white to increase visibility for the dog. You may also want to have an unpainted dumbbell to use on a light-colored floor. Always carry at least two, and preferably three, dumbbells in case one breaks in the ring. If this happens, the judge will have you repeat the throw with an unbroken dumbbell. Keep your spare at your seat at ringside or on the table at the ring entrance so it is readily available. If your dog has chewed up the dowel of your practice dumbbell in training, get an additional unchewed dumbbell to use in the ring. Ask your instructor how to stop the dog from chewing and mouthing the dumbbell. Be sure the dog has had a few opportunities to retrieve the new dumbbell so it is not strange to him in the ring. Handing the judge a chewed-on dumbbell in the ring unnecessarily telegraphs your training problem and could cause him to watch more closely to catch the dog mouthing the dumbbell, and make a deduction.

It is important that you practice throwing the dumbbell so you can place it to your dog's advantage in the ring. Ideally, the dog should retrieve under any circumstances, but it is helpful to keep him away from a spot where another dog fouled the ring (an invitation

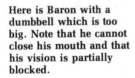

Here is Baron with a dumbbell which is too big. Note that he cannot close his mouth and that his vision is partially blocked.

to sniff, or worse) or an area at ringside where spectators are noisily eating lunch. (If such people are especially close to the ring barrier, you may ask the steward to request that they move a bit further away before you enter the ring). Be sure to practice having to re-throw the dumbbell with your dog. Some dogs have a problem with anticipating the retrieve in case of a re-throw.

Many exhibitors like to give their dog a look at the dumbell (also known as a "mark") before they throw it. This serves to focus the dog's attention so that he will follow the dumbbell with his eyes to the spot where it lands. The mark must be given before you tell the judge you are ready. You may not give your stay signal with the hand that is holding the dumbbell.

Handicapped handlers who cannot throw the dumbbell the required 20-foot distance may leave the dog at the place where the exercise begins, proceed away from the dog however far they must go, and then throw (not drop) the dumbbell. They then return to heel position and proceed with the retrieve exercise in the usual manner.

Pass or Fail? - If your dog waited for the retrieve command, went out on your first command, picked up the dumbbell and brought it back within an arm's length of you, he probably passed. Dogs commonly lose points for moving slowly, not going directly to the dumbbell or returning directly to the handler, dropping the dumbbell or mouthing it. A dog who hits the dumbbell with his feet before picking it up will lose points. No regulation requires a deduction for picking up the dumbbell by the end rather than the dowel. Touching the handler with the dumbbell while sitting in front is also a reason for a minor deduction. Dogs who are new to the Open ring will frequently jump over the high jump in one or both directions in the course of this exercise. This is especially likely if the ring is small and/or the handler throws the dumbbell close to the jump. This calls for a substantial penalty for not returning directly, but should *not* result in a non-qualifying score.

A dog who drops the dumbbell at any time will be penalized. If he drops it in front of the handler, it must be within the handler's reach (without his having to move either foot) to qualify.

THE RETRIEVE OVER THE HIGH JUMP

All of the discussion of the retrieve on the flat pertains equally to this exercise. There are some additional considerations regarding the high jump. You and the dog must stand at least eight feet back from the jump. Frequently, the judge will have drawn some sort of line on the floor or mat at the eight foot mark. Many dogs, however, do better if given more room to run up to the jump. You may want to experiment with your dog to see what distance is best for him. You can frequently get as far as 15 feet or more from the jump. If you have trouble judging distance visually, you can simply figure out ahead of time how many steps you must take to measure off the desired distance, and then, while in the ring, unobtrusively pace off that number of steps before facing the jump.

You must also discover whether your dog does better when you center him in front of the jump, or when you center yourself. In the former case, some dogs will be less likely to run around the left side of the jump. Centering yourself, however, increases the odds for a straight sit in front. Handlers have a tendency to move their feet after sending the dog for the dumbbell. As in the recall, this is a handling error. Adjust your position before you tell the judge you are ready and then stand still.

As in the retrieve on the flat, the accuracy of your throw is important. In fact, it may mean the difference between the dog's passing or failing. Most dogs will consistently turn in one direction (right or left) after picking up the dumbbell and before coming back to you. If your dog turns to the right and you have thrown the dumbbell to the right of the jump, the dog will be looking directly at you rather than at the jump when he turns after picking up the dumbbell. He is more likely to bypass the jump on the return than if you had centered your throw or even thrown a bit toward the left. Observe your dog and take his turn direction into consideration. You should, of course, proof train your dog to jump in both directions, no matter where the dumbbell lands. Discuss this with your instructor. You must throw the dumbbell at least eight feet beyond the jump.

A dog who climbs the jump—that is, puts his front or back feet on top of the jump and pushes off—will fail this exercise. A dog who merely touches the jump, even if it is a hard touch, will probably not fail, but will lose points. If your dog hits the jump hard enough to knock it over, he will also fail.

Pass or Fail? - If the dog waited for your command, left on the first command, jumped in both directions and returned with the dumbbell, he probably passed. On more than one occasion a dog has dropped the dumbbell before the return jump, and with no additional command from the handler has realized his error and jumped back over the jump, picked up the dumbbell and completed the retrieve over the jump again. Most judges will qualify the dog who does this although many points will be lost.

THE BROAD JUMP

As with the high jump, starting the dog consistently from the same distance may be beneficial, keeping in mind the eight-foot minimum. Some exhibitors prefer to position their dogs to the left of the center of the jump rather than centering the dog in front of the jump. This is supposed to prevent the dog from cutting the right corner when he jumps.

After leaving the dog, the handler must stand facing the side of the jump, two feet back from it. You may choose to stand anywhere between the low edge of the first board and the high edge of the last board. Practice standing in different spots to see which position allows the dog to sit straight in front without cutting the corner of the jump as he turns. *You must turn to your right while the dog is in mid-air.* Do not overturn to compensate for your dog's overly wide return circle. Many exhibitors whose dogs usually finish to the left, teach their dog to finish to the right for this exercise. Larger dogs especially may have difficulty finishing to the left in the rather small area between the handler and the jump.

The most common handling errors on this exercise are the use of body English when sending the dog and failure to make the turn correctly and smoothly.

Note the timing of the turn, beginning while the dog is in mid-air. The author and Belgian Tervuren Ch. & O.T. Ch. Fern Hill Act One T.D.

Pass or Fail? - If the dog waits for your command, goes on the first command, clears all the boards in the jump with its forelegs and returns within arm's reach, he will probably pass. Dogs lose points for ticking the last board with their rear legs, for cutting the right corner (if this is severe enough, the dog may fail), for returning slowly and for making a wide circle rather than returning directly to the handler. A dog who makes an extremely wide return circle in a small ring may find himself in front of the high jump. If he jumps the high jump and still manages to get within the handler's reach without any additional command, he should pass, although he will lose many points. This is a surprisingly common occurrence in the Open Ring.

THE OPEN GROUP EXERCISES

The rules governing the three-minute out-of-sight Long Sit and the five-minute Long Down are essentially the same as for the Novice group exercises. Pay attention to the people on either side of you, so you can find your place in the line before the group returns from its hidden position. Keep track of the time that has elapsed, not to outguess the judge, but to have an idea of when to line up for the return.

At one trial, an exhibitor wandered away from the group and did not notice when the handlers were called back to the ring. The judge was certainly surprised to find one dog left over when the exercise was finished. (A steward was sent in search of the absent-minded exhibitor.)

If a dog bolts from the ring while the handlers are out of sight or if he shows aggression toward a steward or another dog, the judge or steward will attempt to catch or remove the dog. If this is not possible the judge will have the handler called back to the ring before the designated time period has elapsed to collect the dog. Again, listen closely to the judge's instructions so you will know what to do if you return to find there is only an empty space where you had left your dog. Remember not to correct your dog for changing position on either exercise, no matter how tempted you are to do so.

The criteria for passing or failing are exactly the same as for the Novice group exercises.

Chapter 6

The Utility Ring

All of the information pertaining to entering the Open ring (see page 48) applies equally to the Utility ring, except that you will report only one jump height.

THE SIGNAL EXERCISE

As was explained under the Drop on Recall, AKC Regulations describe only the signal for downing the dog. Other signals can be devised at the handler's discretion, with certain restrictions. Signals may be given with the hand and arm only. No additional body movements are permitted except that the handler may bend his body and knees to give a signal at the dog's eye level when the dog is in heel position. This means that you may bend down to your Chihuahua, but your signal must not touch the dog. Signals must be silent. All signals must consist of a single gesture—not a series of jerky movements around the handler's head and body—and the signaling arm must be immediately returned to a natural position at the handler's side. Observe yourself giving signals in a mirror, or have somebody film you to be sure your signals meet these requirements. Strive to keep your signals the same each time you give them. It is also advisable to be sure your signals for the different parts of the exercise appear distinct to the dog. Some exhibitors use a series of nearly identical gestures, which must be confusing to the dog. Check with your instructor. Handicapped handlers who have limited use of their hands and arms may make arrangements with the judge, well before it is their turn in the ring, to signal with some other part of the body. They should show the judge the signals they intend to use so that he has a basis on which to judge the dog's response.

The Regulations clearly state that signals may not be held or the team will fail the exercise. However, you may want to consider holding a signal for a few seconds if the dog looks away just as you begin a signal. If the dog responds as soon as he looks back at you the judge may choose to make a very substantial deduction, but may pass the dog. This is an individual judgment call which will vary from judge to judge. Similarly, if the dog becomes distracted immediately after the judge has indicated that you are to give a particular signal, you would be wise to wait until the dog looks at you before giving your signal. This is another judgment call, but you will lose points for waiting under any circumstances. In both of these cases, you really have nothing to lose by waiting and may squeak by with a qualifying score.

The most common handling errors seen in this exercise are the use of body English, giving verbal commands on the heeling portion of the exercise, holding signals when the dog is watching (and simply not responding), and taking too many steps forward before obeying the command "Stand your dog."

Pass or Fail? - If the dog performed the heeling portion adequately and then waited for and responded to the first signals to stand, stay, down, sit and come, and did not move forward more than about a body length while progressing through the first four signals, he probably passed. If the dog responded slowly to any signal or walked forward a few steps, he will lose points. A verbal command to heel or finish will result in a substantial deduction, but not necessarily a failure.

SCENT DISCRIMINATION

The requirements regarding the scent articles are clearly spelled out in the Regulations. Exhibitors use a wide range of objects as well as the ready-made sets which are sold by various pet supply firms. Baby shoes, tuna cans, rolled leather scraps, and bent spoons have all been used as scent articles. As long as they are no more than six inches long and are clearly numbered, you may use any items that fit the description in the Regulations. The handler must use only his hands to scent the article. Some judges will permit the handler to begin scenting the first acticle while he and the dog are watching the articles being placed and scented by the steward. Other judges do not permit you to scent the first article until you have turned your back to the article pile.

It is permissible to give the dog the "mark" command or otherwise focus his attention while the steward is laying out the articles. Be sure you do not touch the dog as you do this. You may choose to give the dog the scent before sending him by touching his nose with your open hand. Some trainers feel that touching the dog's nose overwhelms him with scent, and prefer to keep their hands several inches from the dog's nose. They may choose to give the dog a verbal command to "Smell," as an extra, legal reminder of what comes next. Some trainers eliminate this gesture entirely. Ask your instructor.

You have two options for getting the dog to the articles: to turn and send him directly, or to turn and stop, and then send him to retrieve. The first option gives the dog one less opportunity for a crooked sit, and usually results in a faster approach to the article pile. If the dog has received some kind of retrieve command before the turn, and then stops on his own after the turn, he will fail. Some exhibitors prefer the turn, stop and send because they feel it allows the dog to focus more accurately on the article pile than the other method and because it more closely resembles the retrieve on the flat. With either method, be careful to return your hand to a natural position after giving the scent and before you turn. If you use the turn and send method, you must also be certain that you give your retrieve command *before* you turn.

A handler will lose points on this exercise for looking over his shoulder to watch the scented article being placed, using excessive body English in sending the dog, attempting to control the dog by facial expression while he is smelling the articles, and shuffling his feet around after sending the dog.

Pass or Fail? - If the dog waited for and then went out on the first command, retrieved the right article and brought it back within arm's reach, he probably passed. The dog will lose points for dawdling, gazing into space, and sniffing anything but the pile of articles. He may sniff at the articles for any reasonable time without being penalized, however. Wandering around the ring, or jumping a jump on the way to or from the article pile will be penalized, as will picking up and putting down a wrong article. The Regulations do not specify a penalty for a dog who picks up the correct article, puts it down, smells the other articles again and then retrieves the original correct article. As in the retrieve on the flat, a slow response on any part of this exercise will be penalized.

THE DIRECTED RETRIEVE

The gloves required for this exercise are described as "cotton work gloves" which are predominantly white. The gloves may be all white or may have colored cuffs. If there is a light colored floor with glare from a window or light, the all-white glove may not be as visible as the dark-cuffed glove. Some owners of toy dogs manage to find children's work gloves. The Regulations do not mention the size of the gloves. All gloves should be clean.

The most difficult and critical part of this exercise is the turn toward the desired glove. You may turn to the right or the left for any glove. You will lose points for underturning or overturning, and can also make the retrieve more difficult for the dog. Work with your instructor or your mirror to learn to make smooth turns.

Two signals are permitted on this exercise. In the first, the handler thrusts or swings his left arm forward in a pointing motion and simultaneously gives the retrieve command, and then immediately returns his arm to his side (See page 60). In the second, the handler holds his arm steady along the right side of the dog's head while pointing in the correct direction and then gives the retrieve command (See below). Most judges will penalize a handler who brings his arm alongside the dog's head, pauses a moment and then thrusts his arm forward while giving the retrieve command, as this is not the single gesture called for in the Regulations. Some trainers prefer the steady signal and send (which is more like the "mark" exercise used in retrieving trials, on which this exercise is supposedly based) because it permits them to wait a few seconds before sending the dog. This can be an advantage if the dog initially focused on an incorrect glove as it allows him to correct himself before he is sent. The handler cannot give any help

Gail Clark and Silky Terrier, Tru Blu Pride 'N' Joy, C.D.X., demonstrate the stationary signal. Note the dog and handler's eyes focused on the correct glove.

Here, Gail and her dog demonstrate the moving signal.
Note dog is in motion as the gesture is completed.

in addition to the directional signal. If he waits too long to send the dog, the judge will begin to deduct points and may even fail the dog.

Be sure that you do not give the dog the wrong direction by inadvertently swinging your arm wide when giving the signal. This is a common handling error.

This exercise is the only retrieving exercise in which a signal is required by the Regulations.

Pass or Fail? - In addition to all of the penalties pertinent to the Retrieve on the Flat, in this particular exercise the dog must go *directly* to the correct glove or he will fail. If the dog is sent for glove number two, for instance, and first goes to number one, and then moves across to the correct glove and retrieves it, he will not recieve a qualifying score. Otherwise, scoring for this exercise is identical to the Retrieve on the Flat.

THE DIRECTED JUMPING

The most difficult feature of this exercise from the dog's point of view is the send-away. The idea of going away from the handler in a straight line, especially when there is no bird scent (which lures the field dog forward) is a very abstract concept. Furthermore, many dogs are confused by the previous exercise and when sent away they return to the corner from which they have just retrieved the glove. For this reason many trainers practice having the dog take the jumping direction from any point in the ring, even the corner opposite the indicated jump. Ask your instructor.

If your dog does not go out the required minimum distance of ten feet past the jump, but does stop and sit, the judge may tell you to call him to prevent a possible injury from attempting to jump without sufficient take-off room. Or, you may choose to call him regardless of the judge's direction, as he has already failed. If your dog goes out on the send-away portion of this exercise and does not sit, do not give a second command (unless he has already failed a previous exercise) because he may still qualify. Most judges will wait a few seconds to see if the dog will sit, and then will indicate which jump he is to jump over. Dogs who anticipate the turn or the sit will lose points, but will not fail if they have gone the required minimum distance. On rare occasions a dog will stop and sit facing the ring barrier, without turning to face his hander. Regulations call for the dog to have his attention on his handler, so this would require a penalty.

You may wish to use a different command for each jump to help the dog to choose the correct jump. Your jump signal should be given simultaneously with your verbal command. Be careful to use only your hand and arm to signal; do not make obvious head movements, bend your body, or move your feet. You are not required to give both the signal and verbal command and may use only one if it is beneficial to your dog. Again, as in the signal exercise, you may choose to risk holding your jump signal for a few extra seconds if the dog hesitates or appears to be trying to decide which jump to take. You may still qualify, but will, of course, lose some points.

The handler may turn while the dog is in mid-air to line himself up for the dog's return. You are not required to turn, but most trainers believe it assists the dog in making a good sit in front. Be sure not to overturn or move your feet around to accommodate a dog who is ing a wide return circle.

Pass or Fail? - In order to qualify, the dog must do the following things for each half of the exercise: wait for and then go away on the first command, go out between the jumps (if he jumps on the way out, he will fail), go at least ten feet past the jumps, stop and wait for the direction to be given, jump as directed and return within reach of the handler. If he ticks either jump he will lose points, but if he knocks the bar off, he will fail. Dogs also lose points for slow response on any part of the exercise, failing to go the full twenty feet away, not stopping in the center of the ring, and failing to return directly to the handler. The farther the dog stops from the ideal centered, twenty-foot mark, the more points he will lose.

THE GROUP EXAMINATION (THE LONG STAND)

Some exhibitors pose their dogs in an exaggerated show stance which is difficult for the dog to maintain. Or, they insist that the dog stand perfectly square, with all of his feet aligned. Experiment with your dog to see which position is comfortable for him. Even if his chosen position looks awkward to you, if he will stand steadily in that position there is no need to force him to change. Prepare your dog for any kind of an examination, including having his mouth opened and his testicles handled as in the breed ring. If you encounter a judge who is unfamiliar with the current Regulations (which forbid the last two items), your dog will be prepared. Dogs should also become accustomed to having their feet and tails handled while on the stand stay.

As in the other group exercises, pay attention to the spot you choose to place your dog. At an outdoor show avoid holes and dips which would force him to stand with his weight unbalanced. At an indoor show be sure all of his feet are on the mat.

Pass or Fail? - If your dog remains standing where you left him without repeatedly barking or whining and tolerates the examination (see the discussion of the Novice Stand for Examination), he will probably pass. If he moves a body length or more away, or changes position, he will probably fail. He will lose points for shuffling his feet or for extensive sniffing of the ground. Otherwise, the same rules apply as for the other group exercises.

Reaping The Rewards

THE PLEASURE OF HONEST HANDLING

There is nothing quite as fulfilling as setting a goal, working hard to achieve it and succeeding. The nice thing about the sport of obedience is that not only do you receive public acknowledgment of your success in the form of certificates, ribbons, trophies, and ratings, but you also wind up with a dog who is a delightful pet and with whom you have a deep, mutually beneficial understanding. Those few exhibitors who "nudge" the rules, and those who frankly cheat, even if they are not caught, rob themselves of some of this pleasure and cheapen the sport for everyone.

While the exhibitor who cheats may fool some judges, he cannot fool himself or fellow exhibitors. He may gain a number of additional trophies for his collection, but he will eventually lose the respect of the obedience community. It has been my experience that dishonest exhibitors come to be ostracized by that community.

GIVING BACK TO THE SPORT

If you have derived pleasure from training and showing in obedience, consider putting forth some effort to make the sport accessible to others. Join an obedience club or an all-breed club (they always need obedience enthusiasts) and volunteer to help put on their next match or show. Offer to take on one of the many tasks involved. Make yourself available to judge at a local fun match. (This is how many AKC judges get started.) Help the club run its training classes, if any.

Your trained dog can also be the centerpiece for discussions about responsible pet ownership with friends or public groups. Some exhibitors give presentations at local schools or work with Scout groups. Your titled dog may be eligible to become a Therapy Dog, to be used to bring joy to elderly and/or handicapped residents in nursing homes or other institutions. Check around in your area to see if training classes are offered for the disabled and their dogs; extra hands are always welcome. You may volunteer to help at a local guide dog school or one of the new places which train dogs for the hearing impaired. You will probably not do any actual training of such dogs, but may be needed to help care for them, to socialize puppies, etc. The local Humane Society also has many uses for knowledgeable volunteers.

You don't have to be an expert trainer or have a dog who always scores 198 to participate in these activities. A person who has trained and shown even one dog to a C.D. has many times the knowledge of the average pet owner. Use your imagination to make the skills you have acquired bring pleasure and information to others. You will find that the adage about casting your bread upon the waters also holds true for kibble.

Finally, remain flexible. The most successful trainers are not the ones who have success with only one dog, and who eventually disappear because they could never achieve the same success with subsequent dogs. Nor are they the people who discard dogs like used kleenex when the dogs do not win. The successful trainers and exhibitors enjoy the sport of obedience as a learning experience, an opportunity for personal growth. Whether each new dog is a big winner or merely qualifies, training him is a fresh challenge. Every year brings new friends and new relationships, as well as new ideas. Obedience is a sport for everyone, because everyone can be a winner, canine and human alike.

Appendix

IMPORTANT ADDRESSES

American Kennel Club (AKC)
51 Madison Avenue
New York, New York 10010

Brown County Mixed Breed
Kennel Club
P.O. Box 51/dog
Helmsburg, IN 47435

NEON
P.O. Box 105
Chicopee, MA 01021
This organization awards titles to
dogs who compete in matches
(mixed breeds, non-registered
purebreds, etc.)

LICENSED SUPERINTENDENTS

Antypas, William G.
P.O. Box 7131
Pasadena, CA 91109

Bird, William A.
52 Garfield Lane
Napa, CA 94558

Bradshaw, Jack
P.O. Box 7303
Los Angeles, CA 90022

Brown, Norman E.
P.O. Box 2566
Spokane, WA 99220

Crowe, Thomas J.
P.O. Box 22107
Greensboro, NC 27420

Matthews, Ace H.
P.O. Box 06150
Portland, OR 97206

Onofrio, Jack
P.O. Box 25764
Oklahoma City, OK 73125

Randolph, Mrs. Nora
P.O. Box 16038
San Francisco, CA 94116

Rau, James A., Jr.
P.O. Box 4038
4707 Perkiomen Avenue
Reading, PA 19606

Roberts, B. Jeannie
P.O. Box 31017
Seattle, WA 98103

Sleeper, Kenneth A.
P.O. Box 307
Garrett, IN 46738

Sweet, Mrs. Dorthy G.
2321 Blanco Road
San Antonio, TX 78212